MW01228751

This study guide was created to help you process your thoughts, write down important verses, allow you to think about how the verses relate to your life for retention, and write short notes for each chapter as you are studying the bible. Enjoy the journey!

-R. Parker

The Gospels

Matthew

Chapter 1

MY INTERPRETATION OF VERSES...

VERSES THAT STOOD OUT TO ME

NOTES

HOW THIS CHAPTER RELATES TO MY LIFE

Matthew

Chapter 2

MY INTERPRETATION OF VERSES...

VERSES THAT STOOD OUT TO ME

NOTES

HOW THIS CHAPTER RELATES TO MY LIFE

Matthew

Chapter 3

MY INTERPRETATION OF VERSES...

VERSES THAT STOOD OUT TO ME

NOTES

HOW THIS CHAPTER RELATES TO MY LIFE

Matthew

Chapter 4

MY INTERPRETATION OF VERSES...

VERSES THAT STOOD OUT TO ME

NOTES

HOW THIS CHAPTER RELATES TO MY LIFE

Matthew

Chapter 5

MY INTERPRETATION OF VERSES...

VERSES THAT STOOD OUT TO ME

NOTES

HOW THIS CHAPTER RELATES TO MY LIFE

Matthew

Chapter 6

MY INTERPRETATION OF VERSES...

VERSES THAT STOOD OUT TO ME

NOTES

HOW THIS CHAPTER RELATES TO MY LIFE

Matthew

Chapter 7

MY INTERPRETATION OF VERSES...

VERSES THAT STOOD OUT TO ME

NOTES

HOW THIS CHAPTER RELATES TO MY LIFE

Matthew

Chapter 8

MY INTERPRETATION OF VERSES...

VERSES THAT STOOD OUT TO ME

NOTES

HOW THIS CHAPTER RELATES TO MY LIFE

Matthew

Chapter 9

MY INTERPRETATION OF VERSES...

VERSES THAT STOOD OUT TO ME

NOTES

HOW THIS CHAPTER RELATES TO MY LIFE

Matthew

Chapter 10

MY INTERPRETATION OF VERSES...

VERSES THAT STOOD OUT TO ME

NOTES

HOW THIS CHAPTER RELATES TO MY LIFE

Matthew

Chapter 11

MY INTERPRETATION OF VERSES...

VERSES THAT STOOD OUT TO ME

NOTES

HOW THIS CHAPTER RELATES TO MY LIFE

Matthew

Chapter 12

MY INTERPRETATION OF VERSES...

VERSES THAT STOOD OUT TO ME

NOTES

HOW THIS CHAPTER RELATES TO MY LIFE

Matthew

Chapter 13

MY INTERPRETATION OF VERSES...

VERSES THAT STOOD OUT TO ME

NOTES

HOW THIS CHAPTER RELATES TO MY LIFE

Matthew

Chapter 14

MY INTERPRETATION OF VERSES...

VERSES THAT STOOD OUT TO ME

NOTES

HOW THIS CHAPTER RELATES TO MY LIFE

Matthew

Chapter 15

MY INTERPRETATION OF VERSES...

VERSES THAT STOOD OUT TO ME

NOTES

HOW THIS CHAPTER RELATES TO MY LIFE

Matthew

Chapter 16

MY INTERPRETATION OF VERSES...

VERSES THAT STOOD OUT TO ME

NOTES

HOW THIS CHAPTER RELATES TO MY LIFE

Matthew

Chapter 17

MY INTERPRETATION OF VERSES...

VERSES THAT STOOD OUT TO ME

NOTES

HOW THIS CHAPTER RELATES TO MY LIFE

Matthew

Chapter 18

MY INTERPRETATION OF VERSES...

VERSES THAT STOOD OUT TO ME

NOTES

HOW THIS CHAPTER RELATES TO MY LIFE

Matthew

Chapter 19

MY INTERPRETATION OF VERSES...

VERSES THAT STOOD OUT TO ME

NOTES

HOW THIS CHAPTER RELATES TO MY LIFE

Matthew

Chapter 20

MY INTERPRETATION OF VERSES...

VERSES THAT STOOD OUT TO ME

NOTES

HOW THIS CHAPTER RELATES TO MY LIFE

Matthew

Chapter 21

MY INTERPRETATION OF VERSES...

VERSES THAT STOOD OUT TO ME

NOTES

HOW THIS CHAPTER RELATES TO MY LIFE

Matthew

Chapter 22

MY INTERPRETATION OF VERSES...

VERSES THAT STOOD OUT TO ME

NOTES

HOW THIS CHAPTER RELATES TO MY LIFE

Matthew

Chapter 23

MY INTERPRETATION OF VERSES...

VERSES THAT STOOD OUT TO ME

NOTES

HOW THIS CHAPTER RELATES TO MY LIFE

Matthew

Chapter 24

MY INTERPRETATION OF VERSES...

VERSES THAT STOOD OUT TO ME

NOTES

HOW THIS CHAPTER RELATES TO MY LIFE

Matthew

Chapter 25

MY INTERPRETATION OF VERSES...

VERSES THAT STOOD OUT TO ME

NOTES

HOW THIS CHAPTER RELATES TO MY LIFE

Matthew

Chapter 26

MY INTERPRETATION OF VERSES...

VERSES THAT STOOD OUT TO ME

NOTES

HOW THIS CHAPTER RELATES TO MY LIFE

Matthew

Chapter 27

MY INTERPRETATION OF VERSES...

VERSES THAT STOOD OUT TO ME

NOTES

HOW THIS CHAPTER RELATES TO MY LIFE

Matthew

Chapter 28

MY INTERPRETATION OF VERSES...

VERSES THAT STOOD OUT TO ME

NOTES

HOW THIS CHAPTER RELATES TO MY LIFE

Mark

Chapter 1

MY INTERPRETATION OF VERSES...

VERSES THAT STOOD OUT TO ME

NOTES

HOW THIS CHAPTER RELATES TO MY LIFE

Mark

Chapter 2

MY INTERPRETATION OF VERSES...

VERSES THAT STOOD OUT TO ME

NOTES

HOW THIS CHAPTER RELATES TO MY LIFE

Mark

Chapter 3

MY INTERPRETATION OF VERSES...

VERSES THAT STOOD OUT TO ME

NOTES

HOW THIS CHAPTER RELATES TO MY LIFE

Mark

Chapter 4

MY INTERPRETATION OF VERSES...

VERSES THAT STOOD OUT TO ME

NOTES

HOW THIS CHAPTER RELATES TO MY LIFE

Mark

Chapter 5

MY INTERPRETATION OF VERSES...

VERSES THAT STOOD OUT TO ME

NOTES

HOW THIS CHAPTER RELATES TO MY LIFE

Mark

Chapter 6

MY INTERPRETATION OF VERSES...

VERSES THAT STOOD OUT TO ME

NOTES

HOW THIS CHAPTER RELATES TO MY LIFE

Mark

Chapter 7

MY INTERPRETATION OF VERSES...

VERSES THAT STOOD OUT TO ME

NOTES

HOW THIS CHAPTER RELATES TO MY LIFE

MARK

Chapter 8

MY INTERPRETATION OF VERSES...

VERSES THAT STOOD OUT TO ME

NOTES

HOW THIS CHAPTER RELATES TO MY LIFE

Mark

Chapter 9

MY INTERPRETATION OF VERSES...

VERSES THAT STOOD OUT TO ME

NOTES

HOW THIS CHAPTER RELATES TO MY LIFE

Mark

Chapter 10

MY INTERPRETATION OF VERSES...

VERSES THAT STOOD OUT TO ME

NOTES

HOW THIS CHAPTER RELATES TO MY LIFE

Mark

Chapter 11

MY INTERPRETATION OF VERSES...

VERSES THAT STOOD OUT TO ME

NOTES

HOW THIS CHAPTER RELATES TO MY LIFE

Mark

Chapter 12

MY INTERPRETATION OF VERSES...

VERSES THAT STOOD OUT TO ME

NOTES

HOW THIS CHAPTER RELATES TO MY LIFE

Mark

Chapter 13

MY INTERPRETATION OF VERSES...

VERSES THAT STOOD OUT TO ME

NOTES

HOW THIS CHAPTER RELATES TO MY LIFE

Mark

Chapter 14

MY INTERPRETATION OF VERSES...

VERSES THAT STOOD OUT TO ME

NOTES

HOW THIS CHAPTER RELATES TO MY LIFE

Mark

Chapter 15

MY INTERPRETATION OF VERSES...

VERSES THAT STOOD OUT TO ME

NOTES

HOW THIS CHAPTER RELATES TO MY LIFE

Mark

Chapter 16

MY INTERPRETATION OF VERSES...

VERSES THAT STOOD OUT TO ME

NOTES

HOW THIS CHAPTER RELATES TO MY LIFE

Luke

Chapter 1

MY INTERPRETATION OF VERSES...

VERSES THAT STOOD OUT TO ME

NOTES

HOW THIS CHAPTER RELATES TO MY LIFE

Luke

Chapter 2

MY INTERPRETATION OF VERSES...

VERSES THAT STOOD OUT TO ME

NOTES

HOW THIS CHAPTER RELATES TO MY LIFE

Luke

Chapter 3

MY INTERPRETATION OF VERSES...

VERSES THAT STOOD OUT TO ME

NOTES

HOW THIS CHAPTER RELATES TO MY LIFE

Luke

Chapter 4

MY INTERPRETATION OF VERSES...

VERSES THAT STOOD OUT TO ME

NOTES

HOW THIS CHAPTER RELATES TO MY LIFE

Luke

Chapter 5

MY INTERPRETATION OF VERSES...

VERSES THAT STOOD OUT TO ME

NOTES

HOW THIS CHAPTER RELATES TO MY LIFE

Luke

Chapter 6

MY INTERPRETATION OF VERSES...

VERSES THAT STOOD OUT TO ME

NOTES

HOW THIS CHAPTER RELATES TO MY LIFE

Luke

Chapter 7

MY INTERPRETATION OF VERSES...

VERSES THAT STOOD OUT TO ME

NOTES

HOW THIS CHAPTER RELATES TO MY LIFE

Luke

Chapter 8

MY INTERPRETATION OF VERSES...

VERSES THAT STOOD OUT TO ME

NOTES

HOW THIS CHAPTER RELATES TO MY LIFE

Luke

Chapter 9

MY INTERPRETATION OF VERSES...

VERSES THAT STOOD OUT TO ME

NOTES

HOW THIS CHAPTER RELATES TO MY LIFE

Luke

Chapter 10

MY INTERPRETATION OF VERSES...

VERSES THAT STOOD OUT TO ME

NOTES

HOW THIS CHAPTER RELATES TO MY LIFE

Luke

Chapter 11

MY INTERPRETATION OF VERSES...

VERSES THAT STOOD OUT TO ME

NOTES

HOW THIS CHAPTER RELATES TO MY LIFE

Luke

Chapter 12

MY INTERPRETATION OF VERSES...

VERSES THAT STOOD OUT TO ME

NOTES

HOW THIS CHAPTER RELATES TO MY LIFE

Luke

Chapter 13

MY INTERPRETATION OF VERSES...

VERSES THAT STOOD OUT TO ME

NOTES

HOW THIS CHAPTER RELATES TO MY LIFE

Luke

Chapter 14

MY INTERPRETATION OF VERSES...

VERSES THAT STOOD OUT TO ME

NOTES

HOW THIS CHAPTER RELATES TO MY LIFE

Luke

Chapter 15

MY INTERPRETATION OF VERSES...

VERSES THAT STOOD OUT TO ME

NOTES

HOW THIS CHAPTER RELATES TO MY LIFE

Luke

Chapter 16

MY INTERPRETATION OF VERSES...

VERSES THAT STOOD OUT TO ME

NOTES

HOW THIS CHAPTER RELATES TO MY LIFE

Luke

Chapter 17

MY INTERPRETATION OF VERSES...

VERSES THAT STOOD OUT TO ME

NOTES

HOW THIS CHAPTER RELATES TO MY LIFE

Luke

Chapter 18

MY INTERPRETATION OF VERSES...

VERSES THAT STOOD OUT TO ME

NOTES

HOW THIS CHAPTER RELATES TO MY LIFE

Luke

Chapter 19

MY INTERPRETATION OF VERSES...

VERSES THAT STOOD OUT TO ME

NOTES

HOW THIS CHAPTER RELATES TO MY LIFE

Luke

Chapter 20

MY INTERPRETATION OF VERSES...

VERSES THAT STOOD OUT TO ME

NOTES

HOW THIS CHAPTER RELATES TO MY LIFE

Luke

Chapter 21

MY INTERPRETATION OF VERSES...

VERSES THAT STOOD OUT TO ME

NOTES

HOW THIS CHAPTER RELATES TO MY LIFE

Luke

Chapter 22

MY INTERPRETATION OF VERSES...

VERSES THAT STOOD OUT TO ME

NOTES

HOW THIS CHAPTER RELATES TO MY LIFE

Luke

Chapter 23

MY INTERPRETATION OF VERSES...

VERSES THAT STOOD OUT TO ME

NOTES

HOW THIS CHAPTER RELATES TO MY LIFE

Luke

Chapter 24

MY INTERPRETATION OF VERSES...

VERSES THAT STOOD OUT TO ME

NOTES

HOW THIS CHAPTER RELATES TO MY LIFE

John

Chapter 1

MY INTERPRETATION OF VERSES...

VERSES THAT STOOD OUT TO ME

NOTES

HOW THIS CHAPTER RELATES TO MY LIFE

John

Chapter 2

MY INTERPRETATION OF VERSES...

VERSES THAT STOOD OUT TO ME

NOTES

HOW THIS CHAPTER RELATES TO MY LIFE

John

Chapter 3

MY INTERPRETATION OF VERSES...

VERSES THAT STOOD OUT TO ME

NOTES

HOW THIS CHAPTER RELATES TO MY LIFE

John

Chapter 4

MY INTERPRETATION OF VERSES...

VERSES THAT STOOD OUT TO ME

NOTES

HOW THIS CHAPTER RELATES TO MY LIFE

John

Chapter 5

MY INTERPRETATION OF VERSES...

VERSES THAT STOOD OUT TO ME

NOTES

HOW THIS CHAPTER RELATES TO MY LIFE

John

Chapter 6

MY INTERPRETATION OF VERSES...

VERSES THAT STOOD OUT TO ME

NOTES

HOW THIS CHAPTER RELATES TO MY LIFE

John

Chapter 7

MY INTERPRETATION OF VERSES...

VERSES THAT STOOD OUT TO ME

NOTES

HOW THIS CHAPTER RELATES TO MY LIFE

John

Chapter 8

MY INTERPRETATION OF VERSES...

VERSES THAT STOOD OUT TO ME

NOTES

HOW THIS CHAPTER RELATES TO MY LIFE

John

Chapter 9

MY INTERPRETATION OF VERSES...

VERSES THAT STOOD OUT TO ME

NOTES

HOW THIS CHAPTER RELATES TO MY LIFE

John

Chapter 10

MY INTERPRETATION OF VERSES...

VERSES THAT STOOD OUT TO ME

NOTES

HOW THIS CHAPTER RELATES TO MY LIFE

John

Chapter 11

MY INTERPRETATION OF VERSES...

VERSES THAT STOOD OUT TO ME

NOTES

HOW THIS CHAPTER RELATES TO MY LIFE

John

Chapter 12

MY INTERPRETATION OF VERSES...

VERSES THAT STOOD OUT TO ME

NOTES

HOW THIS CHAPTER RELATES TO MY LIFE

John

Chapter 13

MY INTERPRETATION OF VERSES...

VERSES THAT STOOD OUT TO ME

NOTES

HOW THIS CHAPTER RELATES TO MY LIFE

John

Chapter 14

MY INTERPRETATION OF VERSES...

VERSES THAT STOOD OUT TO ME

NOTES

HOW THIS CHAPTER RELATES TO MY LIFE

John

Chapter 15

MY INTERPRETATION OF VERSES...

VERSES THAT STOOD OUT TO ME

NOTES

HOW THIS CHAPTER RELATES TO MY LIFE

John

Chapter 16

MY INTERPRETATION OF VERSES...

VERSES THAT STOOD OUT TO ME

NOTES

HOW THIS CHAPTER RELATES TO MY LIFE

John

Chapter 17

MY INTERPRETATION OF VERSES...

VERSES THAT STOOD OUT TO ME

NOTES

HOW THIS CHAPTER RELATES TO MY LIFE

John

Chapter 18

MY INTERPRETATION OF VERSES...

VERSES THAT STOOD OUT TO ME

HOW THIS CHAPTER RELATES TO MY LIFE

NOTES

John

Chapter 19

MY INTERPRETATION OF VERSES...

VERSES THAT STOOD OUT TO ME

NOTES

HOW THIS CHAPTER RELATES TO MY LIFE

John

Chapter 20

MY INTERPRETATION OF VERSES...

VERSES THAT STOOD OUT TO ME

NOTES

HOW THIS CHAPTER RELATES TO MY LIFE

John

Chapter 21

MY INTERPRETATION OF VERSES...

VERSES THAT STOOD OUT TO ME

NOTES

HOW THIS CHAPTER RELATES TO MY LIFE

Acts of the Apostles

Acts

Chapter 1

MY INTERPRETATION OF VERSES...

VERSES THAT STOOD OUT TO ME

NOTES

HOW THIS CHAPTER RELATES TO MY LIFE

Acts

Chapter 2

MY INTERPRETATION OF VERSES...

VERSES THAT STOOD OUT TO ME

NOTES

HOW THIS CHAPTER RELATES TO MY LIFE

Acts

Chapter 3

MY INTERPRETATION OF VERSES...

VERSES THAT STOOD OUT TO ME

NOTES

HOW THIS CHAPTER RELATES TO MY LIFE

Acts

Chapter 4

MY INTERPRETATION OF VERSES...

VERSES THAT STOOD OUT TO ME

NOTES

HOW THIS CHAPTER RELATES TO MY LIFE

Acts

Chapter 5

MY INTERPRETATION OF VERSES...

VERSES THAT STOOD OUT TO ME

NOTES

HOW THIS CHAPTER RELATES TO MY LIFE

Acts

Chapter 6

MY INTERPRETATION OF VERSES...

VERSES THAT STOOD OUT TO ME

NOTES

HOW THIS CHAPTER RELATES TO MY LIFE

Acts

Chapter 7

MY INTERPRETATION OF VERSES...

VERSES THAT STOOD OUT TO ME

NOTES

HOW THIS CHAPTER RELATES TO MY LIFE

Acts

Chapter 8

MY INTERPRETATION OF VERSES...

VERSES THAT STOOD OUT TO ME

NOTES

HOW THIS CHAPTER RELATES TO MY LIFE

Acts

Chapter 9

MY INTERPRETATION OF VERSES...

VERSES THAT STOOD OUT TO ME

NOTES

HOW THIS CHAPTER RELATES TO MY LIFE

Acts

Chapter 10

MY INTERPRETATION OF VERSES...

VERSES THAT STOOD OUT TO ME

NOTES

HOW THIS CHAPTER RELATES TO MY LIFE

Acts

Chapter 11

MY INTERPRETATION OF VERSES...

VERSES THAT STOOD OUT TO ME

NOTES

HOW THIS CHAPTER RELATES TO MY LIFE

Acts

Chapter 12

MY INTERPRETATION OF VERSES...

VERSES THAT STOOD OUT TO ME

NOTES

HOW THIS CHAPTER RELATES TO MY LIFE

Acts

Chapter 13

MY INTERPRETATION OF VERSES...

VERSES THAT STOOD OUT TO ME

NOTES

HOW THIS CHAPTER RELATES TO MY LIFE

Acts

Chapter 14

MY INTERPRETATION OF VERSES...

VERSES THAT STOOD OUT TO ME

NOTES

HOW THIS CHAPTER RELATES TO MY LIFE

Acts

Chapter 15

MY INTERPRETATION OF VERSES...

VERSES THAT STOOD OUT TO ME

HOW THIS CHAPTER RELATES TO MY LIFE

NOTES

Acts

Chapter 16

MY INTERPRETATION OF VERSES...

VERSES THAT STOOD OUT TO ME

NOTES

HOW THIS CHAPTER RELATES TO MY LIFE

Acts

Chapter 17

MY INTERPRETATION OF VERSES...

VERSES THAT STOOD OUT TO ME

NOTES

HOW THIS CHAPTER RELATES TO MY LIFE

Acts

Chapter 18

MY INTERPRETATION OF VERSES...

VERSES THAT STOOD OUT TO ME

NOTES

HOW THIS CHAPTER RELATES TO MY LIFE

Acts

Chapter 19

MY INTERPRETATION OF VERSES...

VERSES THAT STOOD OUT TO ME

NOTES

HOW THIS CHAPTER RELATES TO MY LIFE

Acts

Chapter 20

MY INTERPRETATION OF VERSES...

VERSES THAT STOOD OUT TO ME

NOTES

HOW THIS CHAPTER RELATES TO MY LIFE

Acts

Chapter 21

MY INTERPRETATION OF VERSES...

VERSES THAT STOOD OUT TO ME

NOTES

HOW THIS CHAPTER RELATES TO MY LIFE

Acts

Chapter 22

MY INTERPRETATION OF VERSES...

VERSES THAT STOOD OUT TO ME

NOTES

HOW THIS CHAPTER RELATES TO MY LIFE

Acts

Chapter 23

MY INTERPRETATION OF VERSES...

VERSES THAT STOOD OUT TO ME

NOTES

HOW THIS CHAPTER RELATES TO MY LIFE

Acts

Chapter 24

MY INTERPRETATION OF VERSES...

VERSES THAT STOOD OUT TO ME

NOTES

HOW THIS CHAPTER RELATES TO MY LIFE

Acts

Chapter 25

MY INTERPRETATION OF VERSES...

VERSES THAT STOOD OUT TO ME

NOTES

HOW THIS CHAPTER RELATES TO MY LIFE

Acts

Chapter 26

MY INTERPRETATION OF VERSES...

VERSES THAT STOOD OUT TO ME

NOTES

HOW THIS CHAPTER RELATES TO MY LIFE

Acts

Chapter 27

MY INTERPRETATION OF VERSES...

VERSES THAT STOOD OUT TO ME

NOTES

HOW THIS CHAPTER RELATES TO MY LIFE

Acts

Chapter 28

MY INTERPRETATION OF VERSES...

VERSES THAT STOOD OUT TO ME

NOTES

HOW THIS CHAPTER RELATES TO MY LIFE

The Epistles

Romans

Chapter 1

MY INTERPRETATION OF VERSES...

VERSES THAT STOOD OUT TO ME

NOTES

HOW THIS CHAPTER RELATES TO MY LIFE

Romans

Chapter 2

MY INTERPRETATION OF VERSES...

VERSES THAT STOOD OUT TO ME

NOTES

HOW THIS CHAPTER RELATES TO MY LIFE

Romans

Chapter 3

MY INTERPRETATION OF VERSES...

VERSES THAT STOOD OUT TO ME

NOTES

HOW THIS CHAPTER RELATES TO MY LIFE

Romans

Chapter 4

MY INTERPRETATION OF VERSES...

VERSES THAT STOOD OUT TO ME

NOTES

HOW THIS CHAPTER RELATES TO MY LIFE

Romans

Chapter 5

MY INTERPRETATION OF VERSES...

VERSES THAT STOOD OUT TO ME

NOTES

HOW THIS CHAPTER RELATES TO MY LIFE

Romans

Chapter 6

MY INTERPRETATION OF VERSES...

VERSES THAT STOOD OUT TO ME

NOTES

HOW THIS CHAPTER RELATES TO MY LIFE

Romans

Chapter 7

MY INTERPRETATION OF VERSES...

VERSES THAT STOOD OUT TO ME

NOTES

HOW THIS CHAPTER RELATES TO MY LIFE

Romans

Chapter 8

MY INTERPRETATION OF VERSES...

VERSES THAT STOOD OUT TO ME

NOTES

HOW THIS CHAPTER RELATES TO MY LIFE

Romans

Chapter 9

MY INTERPRETATION OF VERSES...

VERSES THAT STOOD OUT TO ME

NOTES

HOW THIS CHAPTER RELATES TO MY LIFE

Romans

Chapter 10

MY INTERPRETATION OF VERSES...

VERSES THAT STOOD OUT TO ME

NOTES

HOW THIS CHAPTER RELATES TO MY LIFE

Romans

Chapter 11

MY INTERPRETATION OF VERSES...

VERSES THAT STOOD OUT TO ME

NOTES

HOW THIS CHAPTER RELATES TO MY LIFE

Romans

Chapter 12

MY INTERPRETATION OF VERSES...

VERSES THAT STOOD OUT TO ME

NOTES

HOW THIS CHAPTER RELATES TO MY LIFE

Romans

Chapter 13

MY INTERPRETATION OF VERSES...

VERSES THAT STOOD OUT TO ME

NOTES

HOW THIS CHAPTER RELATES TO MY LIFE

Romans

Chapter 14

MY INTERPRETATION OF VERSES...

VERSES THAT STOOD OUT TO ME

NOTES

HOW THIS CHAPTER RELATES TO MY LIFE

Romans

Chapter 15

MY INTERPRETATION OF VERSES...

VERSES THAT STOOD OUT TO ME

NOTES

HOW THIS CHAPTER RELATES TO MY LIFE

Romans

Chapter 16

MY INTERPRETATION OF VERSES...

VERSES THAT STOOD OUT TO ME

NOTES

HOW THIS CHAPTER RELATES TO MY LIFE

1 Corinthians

Chapter 1

MY INTERPRETATION OF VERSES...

VERSES THAT STOOD OUT TO ME

NOTES

HOW THIS CHAPTER RELATES TO MY LIFE

1 Corinthians

Chapter 2

MY INTERPRETATION OF VERSES...

VERSES THAT STOOD OUT TO ME

NOTES

HOW THIS CHAPTER RELATES TO MY LIFE

1 Corinthians

Chapter 3

MY INTERPRETATION OF VERSES...

VERSES THAT STOOD OUT TO ME

NOTES

HOW THIS CHAPTER RELATES TO MY LIFE

1 Corinthians

Chapter 4

MY INTERPRETATION OF VERSES...

VERSES THAT STOOD OUT TO ME

NOTES

HOW THIS CHAPTER RELATES TO MY LIFE

1 Corinthians

Chapter 5

MY INTERPRETATION OF VERSES...

VERSES THAT STOOD OUT TO ME

NOTES

HOW THIS CHAPTER RELATES TO MY LIFE

I Corinthians

Chapter 6

MY INTERPRETATION OF VERSES...

VERSES THAT STOOD OUT TO ME

NOTES

HOW THIS CHAPTER RELATES TO MY LIFE

1 Corinthians

Chapter 7

MY INTERPRETATION OF VERSES...

VERSES THAT STOOD OUT TO ME

NOTES

HOW THIS CHAPTER RELATES TO MY LIFE

1 Corinthians

Chapter 8

MY INTERPRETATION OF VERSES...

VERSES THAT STOOD OUT TO ME

NOTES

HOW THIS CHAPTER RELATES TO MY LIFE

1 Corinthians

Chapter 9

MY INTERPRETATION OF VERSES...

VERSES THAT STOOD OUT TO ME

NOTES

HOW THIS CHAPTER RELATES TO MY LIFE

1 Corinthians

Chapter 10

MY INTERPRETATION OF VERSES...

VERSES THAT STOOD OUT TO ME

NOTES

HOW THIS CHAPTER RELATES TO MY LIFE

1 Corinthians

Chapter 11

MY INTERPRETATION OF VERSES...

VERSES THAT STOOD OUT TO ME

NOTES

HOW THIS CHAPTER RELATES TO MY LIFE

1 Corinthians

Chapter 12

MY INTERPRETATION OF VERSES...

VERSES THAT STOOD OUT TO ME

NOTES

HOW THIS CHAPTER RELATES TO MY LIFE

1 Corinthians

Chapter 13

MY INTERPRETATION OF VERSES...

VERSES THAT STOOD OUT TO ME

NOTES

HOW THIS CHAPTER RELATES TO MY LIFE

1 Corinthians

Chapter 14

MY INTERPRETATION OF VERSES...

VERSES THAT STOOD OUT TO ME

NOTES

HOW THIS CHAPTER RELATES TO MY LIFE

1 Corinthians

Chapter 15

MY INTERPRETATION OF VERSES...

VERSES THAT STOOD OUT TO ME

NOTES

HOW THIS CHAPTER RELATES TO MY LIFE

1 Corinthians

Chapter 16

MY INTERPRETATION OF VERSES...

VERSES THAT STOOD OUT TO ME

NOTES

HOW THIS CHAPTER RELATES TO MY LIFE

2 Corinthians

Chapter 1

MY INTERPRETATION OF VERSES...

VERSES THAT STOOD OUT TO ME

NOTES

HOW THIS CHAPTER RELATES TO MY LIFE

2 Corinthians

Chapter 2

MY INTERPRETATION OF VERSES...

VERSES THAT STOOD OUT TO ME

NOTES

HOW THIS CHAPTER RELATES TO MY LIFE

2 Corinthians

Chapter 3

MY INTERPRETATION OF VERSES...

VERSES THAT STOOD OUT TO ME

NOTES

HOW THIS CHAPTER RELATES TO MY LIFE

2 Corinthians

Chapter 4

MY INTERPRETATION OF VERSES...

VERSES THAT STOOD OUT TO ME

NOTES

HOW THIS CHAPTER RELATES TO MY LIFE

2 Corinthians

Chapter 5

MY INTERPRETATION OF VERSES...

VERSES THAT STOOD OUT TO ME

NOTES

HOW THIS CHAPTER RELATES TO MY LIFE

2 Corinthians

Chapter 6

MY INTERPRETATION OF VERSES...

VERSES THAT STOOD OUT TO ME

NOTES

HOW THIS CHAPTER RELATES TO MY LIFE

2 Corinthians

Chapter 7

MY INTERPRETATION OF VERSES...

VERSES THAT STOOD OUT TO ME

NOTES

HOW THIS CHAPTER RELATES TO MY LIFE

2 Corinthians

Chapter 8

MY INTERPRETATION OF VERSES...

VERSES THAT STOOD OUT TO ME

NOTES

HOW THIS CHAPTER RELATES TO MY LIFE

2 Corinthians

Chapter 9

MY INTERPRETATION OF VERSES...

VERSES THAT STOOD OUT TO ME

NOTES

HOW THIS CHAPTER RELATES TO MY LIFE

2 Corinthians

Chapter 10

MY INTERPRETATION OF VERSES...

VERSES THAT STOOD OUT TO ME

NOTES

HOW THIS CHAPTER RELATES TO MY LIFE

2 Corinthians

Chapter 11

MY INTERPRETATION OF VERSES...

VERSES THAT STOOD OUT TO ME

NOTES

HOW THIS CHAPTER RELATES TO MY LIFE

2 Corinthians

Chapter 12

MY INTERPRETATION OF VERSES...

VERSES THAT STOOD OUT TO ME

NOTES

HOW THIS CHAPTER RELATES TO MY LIFE

2 Corinthians

Chapter 13

MY INTERPRETATION OF VERSES...

VERSES THAT STOOD OUT TO ME

NOTES

HOW THIS CHAPTER RELATES TO MY LIFE

Galatians

Chapter 1

MY INTERPRETATION OF VERSES...

VERSES THAT STOOD OUT TO ME

NOTES

HOW THIS CHAPTER RELATES TO MY LIFE

Chapter 2

MY INTERPRETATION OF VERSES...

VERSES THAT STOOD OUT TO ME

NOTES

HOW THIS CHAPTER RELATES TO MY LIFE

Galatians

Chapter 3

MY INTERPRETATION OF VERSES...

VERSES THAT STOOD OUT TO ME

NOTES

HOW THIS CHAPTER RELATES TO MY LIFE

Galatians

Chapter 4

MY INTERPRETATION OF VERSES...

VERSES THAT STOOD OUT TO ME

NOTES

HOW THIS CHAPTER RELATES TO MY LIFE

Galatians

Chapter 5

MY INTERPRETATION OF VERSES...

VERSES THAT STOOD OUT TO ME

NOTES

HOW THIS CHAPTER RELATES TO MY LIFE

Galatians

Chapter 6

MY INTERPRETATION OF VERSES...

VERSES THAT STOOD OUT TO ME

NOTES

HOW THIS CHAPTER RELATES TO MY LIFE

Ephesians

Chapter 1

MY INTERPRETATION OF VERSES...

VERSES THAT STOOD OUT TO ME

NOTES

HOW THIS CHAPTER RELATES TO MY LIFE

Ephesians

Chapter 2

MY INTERPRETATION OF VERSES...

VERSES THAT STOOD OUT TO ME

NOTES

HOW THIS CHAPTER RELATES TO MY LIFE

Ephesians

Chapter 3

MY INTERPRETATION OF VERSES...

VERSES THAT STOOD OUT TO ME

NOTES

HOW THIS CHAPTER RELATES TO MY LIFE

Ephesians

Chapter 4

MY INTERPRETATION OF VERSES...

VERSES THAT STOOD OUT TO ME

NOTES

HOW THIS CHAPTER RELATES TO MY LIFE

Ephesians

Chapter 5

MY INTERPRETATION OF VERSES...

VERSES THAT STOOD OUT TO ME

NOTES

HOW THIS CHAPTER RELATES TO MY LIFE

Ephesians

Chapter 6

MY INTERPRETATION OF VERSES...

VERSES THAT STOOD OUT TO ME

NOTES

HOW THIS CHAPTER RELATES TO MY LIFE

Philippians

Chapter 1

MY INTERPRETATION OF VERSES...

VERSES THAT STOOD OUT TO ME

NOTES

HOW THIS CHAPTER RELATES TO MY LIFE

Philippians

Chapter 2

MY INTERPRETATION OF VERSES...

VERSES THAT STOOD OUT TO ME

NOTES

HOW THIS CHAPTER RELATES TO MY LIFE

Philippians

Chapter 3

MY INTERPRETATION OF VERSES...

VERSES THAT STOOD OUT TO ME

NOTES

HOW THIS CHAPTER RELATES TO MY LIFE

Philippians

Chapter 4

MY INTERPRETATION OF VERSES...

VERSES THAT STOOD OUT TO ME

NOTES

HOW THIS CHAPTER RELATES TO MY LIFE

Colossians

Chapter 1

MY INTERPRETATION OF VERSES...

VERSES THAT STOOD OUT TO ME

NOTES

HOW THIS CHAPTER RELATES TO MY LIFE

Colossians

Chapter 2

MY INTERPRETATION OF VERSES...

VERSES THAT STOOD OUT TO ME

NOTES

HOW THIS CHAPTER RELATES TO MY LIFE

Colossians

Chapter 3

MY INTERPRETATION OF VERSES...

VERSES THAT STOOD OUT TO ME

NOTES

HOW THIS CHAPTER RELATES TO MY LIFE

Colossians

Chapter 4

MY INTERPRETATION OF VERSES...

VERSES THAT STOOD OUT TO ME

NOTES

HOW THIS CHAPTER RELATES TO MY LIFE

1 Thessalonians

Chapter 1

MY INTERPRETATION OF VERSES...

VERSES THAT STOOD OUT TO ME

NOTES

HOW THIS CHAPTER RELATES TO MY LIFE

1 Thessalonians

Chapter 2

MY INTERPRETATION OF VERSES...

VERSES THAT STOOD OUT TO ME

NOTES

HOW THIS CHAPTER RELATES TO MY LIFE

1 Thessalonians

Chapter 3

MY INTERPRETATION OF VERSES...

VERSES THAT STOOD OUT TO ME

NOTES

HOW THIS CHAPTER RELATES TO MY LIFE

1 Thessalonians

Chapter 4

MY INTERPRETATION OF VERSES...

VERSES THAT STOOD OUT TO ME

NOTES

HOW THIS CHAPTER RELATES TO MY LIFE

1 Thessalonians

Chapter 5

MY INTERPRETATION OF VERSES...

VERSES THAT STOOD OUT TO ME

NOTES

HOW THIS CHAPTER RELATES TO MY LIFE

2 Thessalonians

Chapter 1

MY INTERPRETATION OF VERSES...

VERSES THAT STOOD OUT TO ME

NOTES

HOW THIS CHAPTER RELATES TO MY LIFE

2 Thessalonians

Chapter 2

MY INTERPRETATION OF VERSES...

VERSES THAT STOOD OUT TO ME

NOTES

HOW THIS CHAPTER RELATES TO MY LIFE

2 Thessalonians

Chapter 3

MY INTERPRETATION OF VERSES...

VERSES THAT STOOD OUT TO ME

NOTES

HOW THIS CHAPTER RELATES TO MY LIFE

1 Timothy

Chapter 1

MY INTERPRETATION OF VERSES...

VERSES THAT STOOD OUT TO ME

NOTES

HOW THIS CHAPTER RELATES TO MY LIFE

1 Timothy

Chapter 2

MY INTERPRETATION OF VERSES...

VERSES THAT STOOD OUT TO ME

NOTES

HOW THIS CHAPTER RELATES TO MY LIFE

1 Timothy

Chapter 3

MY INTERPRETATION OF VERSES...

VERSES THAT STOOD OUT TO ME

NOTES

HOW THIS CHAPTER RELATES TO MY LIFE

1 Timothy

Chapter 4

MY INTERPRETATION OF VERSES...

VERSES THAT STOOD OUT TO ME

NOTES

HOW THIS CHAPTER RELATES TO MY LIFE

1 Timothy

Chapter 5

MY INTERPRETATION OF VERSES...

VERSES THAT STOOD OUT TO ME

NOTES

HOW THIS CHAPTER RELATES TO MY LIFE

I Timothy

Chapter 6

MY INTERPRETATION OF VERSES...

VERSES THAT STOOD OUT TO ME

NOTES

HOW THIS CHAPTER RELATES TO MY LIFE

2 Timothy

Chapter 1

MY INTERPRETATION OF VERSES...

VERSES THAT STOOD OUT TO ME

NOTES

HOW THIS CHAPTER RELATES TO MY LIFE

2 Timothy

Chapter 2

MY INTERPRETATION OF VERSES...

VERSES THAT STOOD OUT TO ME

NOTES

HOW THIS CHAPTER RELATES TO MY LIFE

2 Timothy

Chapter 3

MY INTERPRETATION OF VERSES...

VERSES THAT STOOD OUT TO ME

NOTES

HOW THIS CHAPTER RELATES TO MY LIFE

2 Timothy

Chapter 4

MY INTERPRETATION OF VERSES...

VERSES THAT STOOD OUT TO ME

NOTES

HOW THIS CHAPTER RELATES TO MY LIFE

Titus

Chapter 1

MY INTERPRETATION OF VERSES...

VERSES THAT STOOD OUT TO ME

NOTES

HOW THIS CHAPTER RELATES TO MY LIFE

Titus

Chapter 2

MY INTERPRETATION OF VERSES...

VERSES THAT STOOD OUT TO ME

NOTES

HOW THIS CHAPTER RELATES TO MY LIFE

Titus

Chapter 3

MY INTERPRETATION OF VERSES...

VERSES THAT STOOD OUT TO ME

NOTES

HOW THIS CHAPTER RELATES TO MY LIFE

Philemon

Chapter 1

MY INTERPRETATION OF VERSES...

VERSES THAT STOOD OUT TO ME

NOTES

HOW THIS CHAPTER RELATES TO MY LIFE

Hebrews

Chapter 1

MY INTERPRETATION OF VERSES...

VERSES THAT STOOD OUT TO ME

NOTES

HOW THIS CHAPTER RELATES TO MY LIFE

Hebrews

Chapter 2

MY INTERPRETATION OF VERSES...

VERSES THAT STOOD OUT TO ME

NOTES

HOW THIS CHAPTER RELATES TO MY LIFE

Hebrews

Chapter 3

MY INTERPRETATION OF VERSES...

VERSES THAT STOOD OUT TO ME

NOTES

HOW THIS CHAPTER RELATES TO MY LIFE

Hebrews

Chapter 4

MY INTERPRETATION OF VERSES...

VERSES THAT STOOD OUT TO ME

NOTES

HOW THIS CHAPTER RELATES TO MY LIFE

Hebrews

Chapter 5

MY INTERPRETATION OF VERSES...

VERSES THAT STOOD OUT TO ME

NOTES

HOW THIS CHAPTER RELATES TO MY LIFE

Hebrews

Chapter 6

MY INTERPRETATION OF VERSES...

VERSES THAT STOOD OUT TO ME

NOTES

HOW THIS CHAPTER RELATES TO MY LIFE

Hebrews

Chapter 7

MY INTERPRETATION OF VERSES...

VERSES THAT STOOD OUT TO ME

NOTES

HOW THIS CHAPTER RELATES TO MY LIFE

Hebrews

Chapter 8

MY INTERPRETATION OF VERSES...

VERSES THAT STOOD OUT TO ME

NOTES

HOW THIS CHAPTER RELATES TO MY LIFE

Hebrews

Chapter 9

MY INTERPRETATION OF VERSES...

VERSES THAT STOOD OUT TO ME

NOTES

HOW THIS CHAPTER RELATES TO MY LIFE

Hebrews

Chapter 10

MY INTERPRETATION OF VERSES...

VERSES THAT STOOD OUT TO ME

NOTES

HOW THIS CHAPTER RELATES TO MY LIFE

Hebrews

Chapter 11

MY INTERPRETATION OF VERSES...

VERSES THAT STOOD OUT TO ME

NOTES

HOW THIS CHAPTER RELATES TO MY LIFE

Hebrews

Chapter 12

MY INTERPRETATION OF VERSES...

VERSES THAT STOOD OUT TO ME

NOTES

HOW THIS CHAPTER RELATES TO MY LIFE

Hebrews

Chapter 13

MY INTERPRETATION OF VERSES...

VERSES THAT STOOD OUT TO ME

NOTES

HOW THIS CHAPTER RELATES TO MY LIFE

James

Chapter 1

MY INTERPRETATION OF VERSES...

VERSES THAT STOOD OUT TO ME

NOTES

HOW THIS CHAPTER RELATES TO MY LIFE

James

Chapter 2

MY INTERPRETATION OF VERSES...

VERSES THAT STOOD OUT TO ME

NOTES

HOW THIS CHAPTER RELATES TO MY LIFE

James

Chapter 3

MY INTERPRETATION OF VERSES...

VERSES THAT STOOD OUT TO ME

NOTES

HOW THIS CHAPTER RELATES TO MY LIFE

James

Chapter 4

MY INTERPRETATION OF VERSES...

VERSES THAT STOOD OUT TO ME

NOTES

HOW THIS CHAPTER RELATES TO MY LIFE

James

Chapter 5

MY INTERPRETATION OF VERSES...

VERSES THAT STOOD OUT TO ME

NOTES

HOW THIS CHAPTER RELATES TO MY LIFE

1 Peter

Chapter 1

MY INTERPRETATION OF VERSES...

VERSES THAT STOOD OUT TO ME

NOTES

HOW THIS CHAPTER RELATES TO MY LIFE

1 Peter

Chapter 2

MY INTERPRETATION OF VERSES...

VERSES THAT STOOD OUT TO ME

NOTES

HOW THIS CHAPTER RELATES TO MY LIFE

1 Peter

Chapter 3

MY INTERPRETATION OF VERSES...

VERSES THAT STOOD OUT TO ME

NOTES

HOW THIS CHAPTER RELATES TO MY LIFE

1 Peter

Chapter 4

MY INTERPRETATION OF VERSES...

VERSES THAT STOOD OUT TO ME

NOTES

HOW THIS CHAPTER RELATES TO MY LIFE

1 Peter

Chapter 5

MY INTERPRETATION OF VERSES...

VERSES THAT STOOD OUT TO ME

NOTES

HOW THIS CHAPTER RELATES TO MY LIFE

2 Peter

Chapter 1

MY INTERPRETATION OF VERSES...

VERSES THAT STOOD OUT TO ME

NOTES

HOW THIS CHAPTER RELATES TO MY LIFE

2 Peter

Chapter 2

MY INTERPRETATION OF VERSES...

VERSES THAT STOOD OUT TO ME

NOTES

HOW THIS CHAPTER RELATES TO MY LIFE

2 Peter

Chapter 3

MY INTERPRETATION OF VERSES...

VERSES THAT STOOD OUT TO ME

NOTES

HOW THIS CHAPTER RELATES TO MY LIFE

I John

Chapter 1

MY INTERPRETATION OF VERSES...

VERSES THAT STOOD OUT TO ME

NOTES

HOW THIS CHAPTER RELATES TO MY LIFE

I John

Chapter 2

MY INTERPRETATION OF VERSES...

VERSES THAT STOOD OUT TO ME

NOTES

HOW THIS CHAPTER RELATES TO MY LIFE

I John

Chapter 3

MY INTERPRETATION OF VERSES...

VERSES THAT STOOD OUT TO ME

NOTES

HOW THIS CHAPTER RELATES TO MY LIFE

I John

Chapter 4

MY INTERPRETATION OF VERSES...

VERSES THAT STOOD OUT TO ME

NOTES

HOW THIS CHAPTER RELATES TO MY LIFE

I John

Chapter 5

MY INTERPRETATION OF VERSES...

VERSES THAT STOOD OUT TO ME

NOTES

HOW THIS CHAPTER RELATES TO MY LIFE

2 John

Chapter 1

MY INTERPRETATION OF VERSES...

VERSES THAT STOOD OUT TO ME

NOTES

HOW THIS CHAPTER RELATES TO MY LIFE

3 John

Chapter 1

MY INTERPRETATION OF VERSES...

VERSES THAT STOOD OUT TO ME

NOTES

HOW THIS CHAPTER RELATES TO MY LIFE

Jude

Chapter 1

MY INTERPRETATION OF VERSES...

VERSES THAT STOOD OUT TO ME

NOTES

HOW THIS CHAPTER RELATES TO MY LIFE

The Apocalypse

Revelation

Chapter 1

MY INTERPRETATION OF VERSES...

VERSES THAT STOOD OUT TO ME

NOTES

HOW THIS CHAPTER RELATES TO MY LIFE

Revelation

Chapter 2

MY INTERPRETATION OF VERSES...

VERSES THAT STOOD OUT TO ME

NOTES

HOW THIS CHAPTER RELATES TO MY LIFE

Revelation

Chapter 3

MY INTERPRETATION OF VERSES...

VERSES THAT STOOD OUT TO ME

NOTES

HOW THIS CHAPTER RELATES TO MY LIFE

Revelation

Chapter 4

MY INTERPRETATION OF VERSES...

VERSES THAT STOOD OUT TO ME

NOTES

HOW THIS CHAPTER RELATES TO MY LIFE

Revelation

Chapter 5

MY INTERPRETATION OF VERSES...

VERSES THAT STOOD OUT TO ME

NOTES

HOW THIS CHAPTER RELATES TO MY LIFE

Revelation

Chapter 6

MY INTERPRETATION OF VERSES...

VERSES THAT STOOD OUT TO ME

NOTES

HOW THIS CHAPTER RELATES TO MY LIFE

Revelation

Chapter 7

MY INTERPRETATION OF VERSES...

VERSES THAT STOOD OUT TO ME

NOTES

HOW THIS CHAPTER RELATES TO MY LIFE

Revelation

Chapter 8

MY INTERPRETATION OF VERSES...

VERSES THAT STOOD OUT TO ME

NOTES

HOW THIS CHAPTER RELATES TO MY LIFE

Revelation

Chapter 9

MY INTERPRETATION OF VERSES...

VERSES THAT STOOD OUT TO ME

NOTES

HOW THIS CHAPTER RELATES TO MY LIFE

Revelation

Chapter 10

MY INTERPRETATION OF VERSES...

VERSES THAT STOOD OUT TO ME

NOTES

HOW THIS CHAPTER RELATES TO MY LIFE

Revelation

Chapter 11

MY INTERPRETATION OF VERSES...

VERSES THAT STOOD OUT TO ME

NOTES

HOW THIS CHAPTER RELATES TO MY LIFE

Revelation

Chapter 12

MY INTERPRETATION OF VERSES...

VERSES THAT STOOD OUT TO ME

NOTES

HOW THIS CHAPTER RELATES TO MY LIFE

Revelation

Chapter 13

MY INTERPRETATION OF VERSES...

VERSES THAT STOOD OUT TO ME

NOTES

HOW THIS CHAPTER RELATES TO MY LIFE

Revelation

Chapter 14

MY INTERPRETATION OF VERSES...

VERSES THAT STOOD OUT TO ME

NOTES

HOW THIS CHAPTER RELATES TO MY LIFE

Revelation

Chapter 15

MY INTERPRETATION OF VERSES...

VERSES THAT STOOD OUT TO ME

NOTES

HOW THIS CHAPTER RELATES TO MY LIFE

Revelation

Chapter 16

MY INTERPRETATION OF VERSES...

VERSES THAT STOOD OUT TO ME

NOTES

HOW THIS CHAPTER RELATES TO MY LIFE

Revelation

Chapter 17

MY INTERPRETATION OF VERSES...

VERSES THAT STOOD OUT TO ME

NOTES

HOW THIS CHAPTER RELATES TO MY LIFE

Revelation

Chapter 18

MY INTERPRETATION OF VERSES...

VERSES THAT STOOD OUT TO ME

NOTES

HOW THIS CHAPTER RELATES TO MY LIFE

Revelation

Chapter 19

MY INTERPRETATION OF VERSES...

VERSES THAT STOOD OUT TO ME

NOTES

HOW THIS CHAPTER RELATES TO MY LIFE

Revelation

Chapter 20

MY INTERPRETATION OF VERSES...

VERSES THAT STOOD OUT TO ME

NOTES

HOW THIS CHAPTER RELATES TO MY LIFE

Revelation

Chapter 21

MY INTERPRETATION OF VERSES...

VERSES THAT STOOD OUT TO ME

NOTES

HOW THIS CHAPTER RELATES TO MY LIFE

Revelation

Chapter 22

MY INTERPRETATION OF VERSES...

VERSES THAT STOOD OUT TO ME

NOTES

HOW THIS CHAPTER RELATES TO MY LIFE

Made in the USA
Columbia, SC
29 July 2024

38894370R30146